Polar Animals

by
David Orme

Thunderbolts

Polar Animals
by David Orme

Illustrated by Michelle Kondrich

Published by Ransom Publishing Ltd.
Radley House, 8 St. Cross Road, Winchester, Hants. SO23 9HX, UK
www.ransom.co.uk

ISBN   978 178127 080 6

First published in 2013

Copyright © 2013 Ransom Publishing Ltd.

Illustrations copyright © 2013 Michelle Kondrich

'Get the Facts' section - images copyright: cover, prelims, passim – Ian Duffy; pp 6/7 - Alan Wilson, Ben Tubby, Brocken Inaglory; pp 8/9 - Teresa, Keith Szafranski; pp 10/11 - Ian Duffy; pp 12/13 - Øystein Paulsen; pp 14/15 - Melissa Madia; pp 16/17 - Chmee2; pp 18/19 - OddurBen, Daniel Benhaim; pp 20/21 - Jason Auch, IronChris; pp 22/23 - Björn Kindler.

A CIP catalogue record of this book is available from the British Library.

All rights reserved. No part of this publication may be reproduced, stored in a retrieval system, or transmitted, in any form or by any means, electronic, mechanical, photocopying, recording or otherwise, without the prior permission of the publishers.

The rights of David Orme to be identified as the author and of Michelle Kondrich to be identified as the illustrator of this Work have been asserted by them in accordance with sections 77 and 78 of the Copyright, Design and Patents Act 1988.

Contents

Polar Animals: The Facts — 5

1. Do polar bears eat penguins? — 6
2. Polar bears — 8
3. Penguins — 10
4. Life under the sea — 12
5. Sea mammals: fact files — 14
6. Land mammals: fact files — 16
7. Amazing journeys – migration — 18
8. How do animals survive in the cold? — 20
9. What about the future? — 22

The Ghost Whale — 25

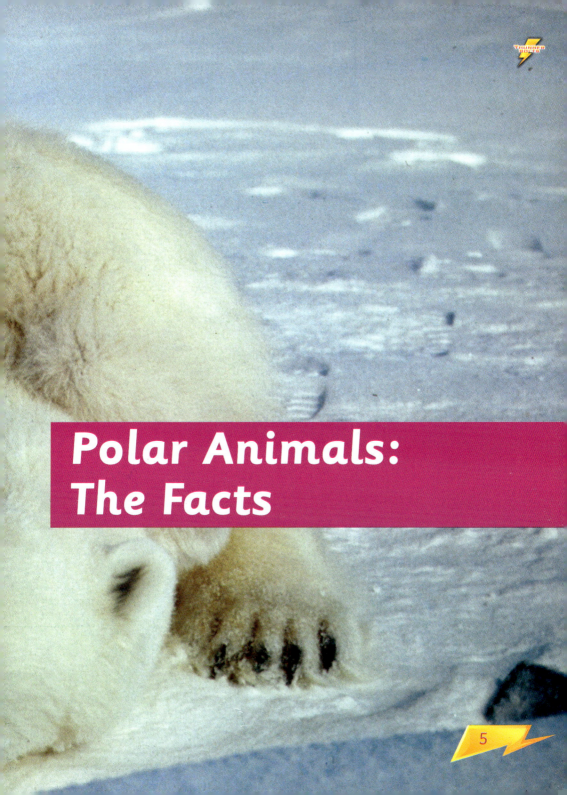
Polar Animals: The Facts

Do polar bears eat penguins?

Of course not!

Polar bears live in the north (the Arctic). Penguins live in the south (the Antarctic). So they never meet.

The Antarctic

The Antarctic is much colder than the Arctic. It is mainly land covered with ice. It has no land mammals.

The Arctic is mainly frozen sea with islands in it. It has land mammals like polar bears and reindeer.

What does the word Arctic mean?

It's a very old word that means 'land of the big bear'.

Polar bears

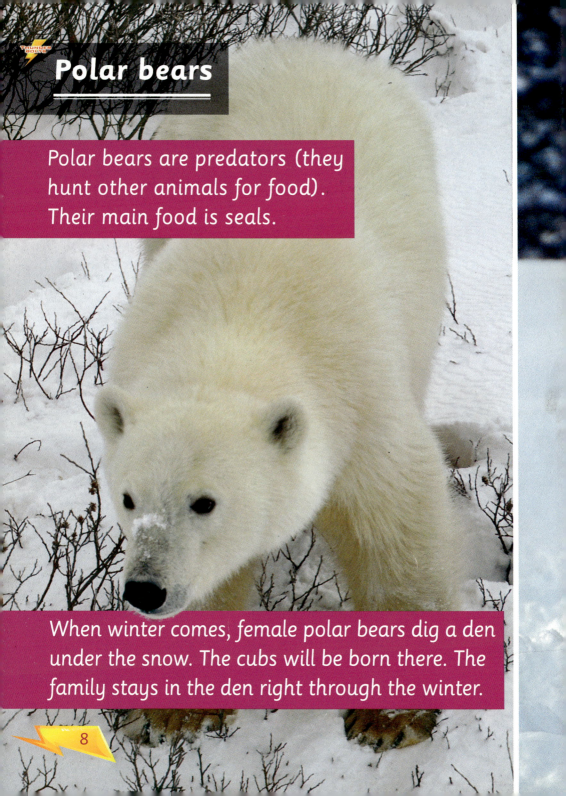

Polar bears are predators (they hunt other animals for food). Their main food is seals.

When winter comes, female polar bears dig a den under the snow. The cubs will be born there. The family stays in the den right through the winter.

In April, the bears come out of the den.

They haven't eaten for months – so they need to get hunting!

Penguins

Penguins can't fly in the air. But they are great at flying under water!

There are different types of penguins, and only some of them live in the Antarctic.

These are Emperor penguins, the biggest type. They like it really cold!

Emperor penguins are great dads. It's their job to keep their egg warm in a special pouch while mum goes off fishing.

They stand in the cold for nine weeks with nothing to eat, waiting for the egg to hatch.

Life under the sea

Life is tough on land in the Arctic and the Antarctic. But the seas are full of life.

These are tiny plants called phytoplankton.

Without them there would be no life in the ocean. They are food for tiny sea creatures called krill.

Krill

Birds, fish and sea mammals feed on krill. If there weren't any phytoplankton, there wouldn't be any krill.

Without krill, there would be no life at all in the oceans.

All these things depend on each other. This is called a food chain.

Sea mammals: fact files

Fact file 1: The killer whale

Also called the orca.

Where it is found: Arctic and Antarctic oceans.

Feeds on: Fish, seals, sea lions, sea birds. They hunt in groups.

Amazing fact: Orcas make many different sounds. Some people think it is a type of language.

Fact file 2: The walrus

Where it is found: Arctic oceans.

Feeds on: Shrimps, crabs and other shellfish.

Amazing fact: Their tusks are used to fight off predators. The most important walrus is the one with the longest tusks!

Land mammals: fact files

Fact file 1: The arctic hare

Where it is found: Arctic islands and the north of Canada.

Feeds on: Twigs, leaves and grass. It has a good sense of smell and can find wood under the snow.

Amazing fact: It can change colour – white in the winter, brown in the summer. This makes it harder for predators to see it.

Fact file 2: The reindeer

Where it is found: Northern Canada, Scandinavia, and Russia.

Feeds on: Leaves and grass, and a plant called reindeer moss.

Amazing fact: Reindeer don't have red noses, but tame ones do pull sleighs!

Amazing journeys – migration

This arctic tern might not look very special, but it is one of the most amazing creatures on Earth.

In the early summer, it lays its eggs in the Arctic. At the end of summer it flies with its new chicks to the edge of the Antarctic.

In their lifetimes arctic terns might fly over two and a half million kilometres!

Minke whales are great travellers too. They are found in all the world's oceans. They can even swim all the way from the Arctic to the Antarctic.

How do animals survive in the cold?

How do animals survive in the Antarctic?

The secret is – lots of layers to keep the heat in!

Whales, seals and penguins have a layer of fat under their skin called blubber.

Penguins have two layers of feathers. Polar bears have two layers of fur, and small ears and noses so they don't lose heat.

Some of the most amazing polar creatures are insects. Their bodies produce a special chemical so they don't freeze. It's the same stuff that people put in their cars in winter!

A woolly bear caterpillar. It won't freeze!

What about the future?

The climate of the world is warming up. People think this is happening because of what we are doing to the Earth.

For polar animals this is mostly bad news.

Polar bears need a frozen sea so they can hunt. They will not be able to catch seals if the ice melts. This is happening already.

Remember that phytoplankton you read about on page 12? Climate change could affect how that grows. That would affect everything that lives in the sea.

What should we do?

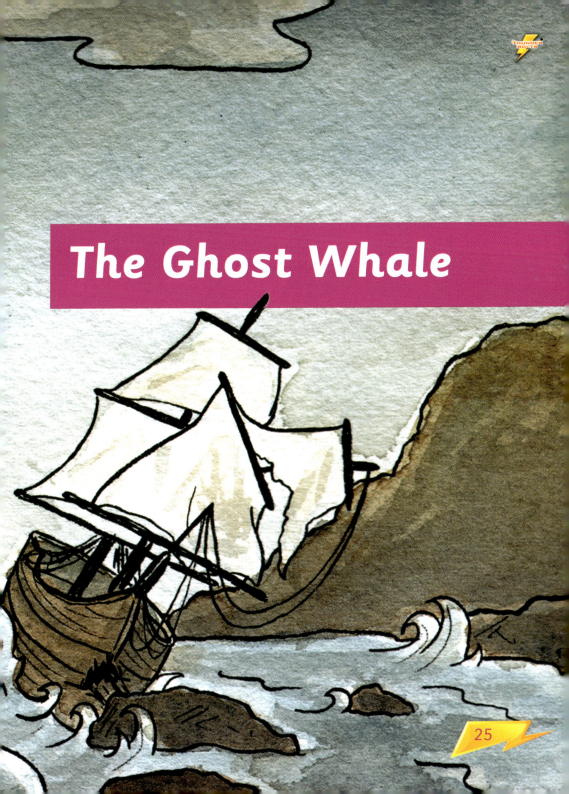
The Ghost Whale

The Ghost Whale 1

It is 1850. Whales are being hunted off the coast of North America.

One morning, the crew of the ship **Mary Bell** sees the biggest whale they have ever seen.

It will make them rich!

The Ghost Whale 2

It was a tough fight, but the whale was killed at last, though two men were drowned.

It was the biggest whale ever caught.

The Ghost Whale   3

A year later the **Mary Bell** was hunting again.

And there was the same whale! Or was it?

The whale turned on the **Mary Bell** and drove it on to the rocks.

Only one man wasn't drowned.

The Ghost Whale   4

The man who lived told everyone his story.

He told them that it was the ghost of the whale that had driven them on to the rocks.

But no one believed him.

The Ghost Whale 5

It is 2013. People are still hunting whales.

The **Greenworld** ship is trying to save the whales. It is a dangerous job.

Suddenly, something huge comes up out of the water!

That whaling ship is in big trouble!

Word list

Antarctic
Arctic
blubber
caterpillar
chemical
climate
Emperor penguin
food chain
ghost
krill
mammal
migration
minke whale
ocean
orca
penguin
phytoplankton
pouch
predator
reindeer
Scandinavia
sleigh
tern
tough